ELEPHANT SKIN FOR BUSINESS

Do it Yourself Step By Step Guide To Unleash your full potential.

By Dr Israel Carlos Lomovasky

Table Of Content

Introduction

Steps to develop elephant skin to succeed in business

1-How do I develop a growth mindset

2-How do I develop self confidence

3-How do I learn from mistakes

4-How do I focus in the big picture

5-How do I develop the ability to take constructive criticism

6-How do I build resilience

7-How do I learn to be persistent

8-How do I practice mindfulness

9-How do I learn to delegate

10-how do I teach myself to stay adaptable

11-How do I learn to set boundaries

12-How do I learn to seek support

13-How do I realize my mental toughness

14-How do I achieve self discipline

Introduction

It is not appropriate to use elephant skin for business purposes, as it is illegal and unethical. The trade of elephant skin and ivory is banned under the Convention on International Trade in Endangered Species (CITES) due to the declining elephant populations caused by poaching.

However, if we take a metaphorical interpretation of "elephant skin for business", it could refer to the thick skin or resilience required in the world of business. In this context, "elephant skin" would mean the ability to withstand criticism, rejection, failure, and other challenges that come with running a business. It is essential to have a thick skin to avoid getting discouraged by negative feedback or setbacks and to remain focused on the ultimate goal.

Building a thick skin in business requires self-confidence, perseverance, and a willingness to learn from mistakes.

Business owners must be able to take constructive criticism and use it to improve their performance, without taking it personally or becoming defensive. They must also be able to handle rejection and failure without losing motivation or giving up.

In conclusion, while using actual elephant skin for business is illegal and unethical, developing a metaphorical "elephant skin" is crucial for success in the world of business. It requires resilience, self-confidence, and a willingness to learn and grow from challenges and setbacks.

Steps to develop elephant skin to succeed in business

Developing a metaphorical "elephant skin" in business can take time, but it is a critical skill for success. Here are some steps that will further up be expanded to help you develop this skill:

1. Cultivate self-confidence: Believing in yourself and your abilities is essential for building a thick skin. Take time to acknowledge your strengths, accomplishments, and successes. Surround yourself with positive and supportive people who can encourage and motivate you.

2. Learn from mistakes: Everyone makes mistakes, but successful business owners use them as opportunities for learning and growth. When you experience setbacks or failures, take time to reflect on what went wrong and what you can do differently in the future.

3. Focus on the big picture: Keeping your eye on the ultimate goal can help you stay motivated and

focused, even when faced with challenges. Remember why you started your business and the impact you hope to make.

4. Take constructive criticism: Receiving feedback, both positive and negative, is essential for growth in business. When receiving criticism, focus on the constructive elements and consider how you can use the feedback to improve your performance.

5. Build resilience: Running a business can be stressful and overwhelming at times, but building resilience can help you stay motivated and focused. Develop healthy coping mechanisms such as exercise, meditation, or spending time with loved ones.

6. Be persistent: Perseverance is key in developing a thick skin. Keep pushing forward, even when faced with rejection or setbacks. Stay committed to your goals, and eventually, you will achieve success.

7. Develop a growth mindset: A growth mindset means embracing challenges and viewing them as opportunities for growth. Emphasize learning and improvement rather than just achieving success, and you'll be able to bounce back from failures and setbacks more easily.

8. Practice mindfulness: Mindfulness can help you stay focused and centered in the face of adversity. Take breaks throughout the day to breathe deeply and be present in the moment. This practice can help you regulate your emotions and react to challenges more calmly.

9. Learn to delegate: Delegating tasks and responsibilities can help you avoid burnout and overwhelm. Surround yourself with a strong team of

employees or contractors and trust them to handle tasks efficiently and effectively.

10. Stay adaptable: Business environments are constantly changing, so it's important to stay flexible and adaptable. Be open to new ideas and approaches and be willing to pivot your strategy if necessary.

11. Set boundaries: It's essential to set boundaries and protect your time and energy. Learn to say "no" to requests or commitments that don't align with your priorities or values.

12. Seek support: Building a successful business can be a lonely journey, so it's crucial to seek support from mentors, peers, or business groups. Connect with like-minded entrepreneurs and share your experiences, challenges, and successes.

By incorporating these additional steps into your business practice, you'll be better equipped to develop a thick skin and succeed in the competitive business world. Remember that building resilience takes time and effort, but with persistence and a growth mindset, you can develop the skills needed to thrive in any situation.

1-How do I develop a growth mindset

Developing a growth mindset requires a willingness to embrace challenges, learn from failures, and persist in the face of obstacles. Here are some steps you can take to develop a growth mindset:

1. Believe in your own potential: Start by recognizing that your abilities and intelligence are not fixed, and that you have the potential to grow and develop through effort and learning.

2. Embrace challenges: Instead of avoiding challenges, seek them out and view them as opportunities for growth and learning. Challenge yourself to learn new skills and take on new responsibilities.

3. Learn from failures: Instead of viewing failure as a setback, see it as a chance to learn and grow. Analyze your mistakes and identify what you can do differently in the future.

4. Practice persistence: Cultivate the persistence to keep going even when faced with obstacles or setbacks. Stay motivated by focusing on your long-term goals and the progress you have already made.

5. Develop a learning mindset: Focus on learning and growth rather than seeking validation or avoiding failure. Embrace a process-oriented approach and be open to feedback and constructive criticism.

6. Surround yourself with positivity: Surround yourself with people who support your growth and development, and avoid negative influences that can hold you back.

7. Be willing to take risks: Growth often requires taking risks and stepping outside your comfort zone. Be willing to take on new challenges and try new things, even if they feel uncomfortable at first.

Remember that developing a growth mindset is a process that takes time and effort. By incorporating these steps into your daily routine and staying focused on your goals, you can cultivate a growth mindset and achieve greater success in all areas of your life.

Here are a few more steps to help you develop a growth mindset:

8. Emphasize effort over talent: Instead of focusing on innate abilities or talent, emphasize the importance of effort and hard work. Recognize that skills and abilities can be

developed through dedicated practice and learning.

9. Use self-reflection: Take time to reflect on your own learning and growth. Keep a journal or use other methods to track your progress and identify areas where you can improve.

10.   Learn from others: Seek out mentors or role models who embody the kind of growth mindset you want to develop. Ask for feedback and learn from their experiences.

11.   Stay open-minded: Be willing to challenge your own assumptions and beliefs. Stay curious and open to new ideas, and be willing to revise your opinions based on new information.

12.   Cultivate a positive attitude: Develop a positive attitude towards challenges and setbacks. Focus on finding solutions and learning from the situation, rather than dwelling on the negative.

13.   Set specific goals: Setting specific goals can help you stay focused on your growth and development. Make sure your goals are challenging, yet achievable, and be willing to adjust them as needed.

14.   Seek out new experiences: Try new things, take on new challenges, and explore new opportunities. This can help you expand your

knowledge and skills, and develop a more

open-minded approach to learning and growth.

15.   Practice self-discipline: Developing a

growth mindset requires discipline and

consistency. Make a habit of practicing the

habits and behaviors that support your growth

and development.

16.   Learn to manage stress: Stress can

interfere with your ability to learn and grow.

Develop strategies to manage stress, such as

exercise, meditation, or deep breathing, to help

you stay focused and productive.

17.   Develop a support system: Surround

yourself with people who support your growth

and development. Seek out mentors, coaches, and peers who can provide guidance and feedback, and who share your values and goals.

Remember that developing a growth mindset is a journey, not a destination. It requires ongoing effort, dedication, and a willingness to learn from your experiences. By incorporating these steps into your daily routine, you can cultivate a growth mindset and achieve greater success in all areas of your life.

2-How do I develop self confidence

Developing self-confidence is a key step in building a metaphorical "elephant skin" and succeeding in business. Here are some specific steps you can take to boost your self-confidence:

1. Identify your strengths: Make a list of your skills, accomplishments, and qualities that you feel proud of. Focus on your positive attributes and recognize the unique value that you bring to your business.

2. Face your fears: Identify the areas where you feel less confident and confront those fears head-on. Take small steps to challenge yourself, whether it's giving a presentation, networking with other business owners, or launching a new product.

3. Practice self-care: Taking care of your physical and emotional needs can help you feel more confident and resilient. Get enough sleep, exercise regularly,

eat a healthy diet, and engage in activities that bring you joy and relaxation.

4. Use positive self-talk: Pay attention to your inner dialogue and replace negative self-talk with positive affirmations. Encourage yourself with phrases like "I can do this" or "I am capable and competent."

5. Learn new skills: Investing in your professional development can help you build confidence and stay competitive. Attend workshops, take courses, or seek out a mentor to learn new skills or strategies.

6. Surround yourself with positivity: Seek out supportive and encouraging people who can offer feedback and help you stay motivated. Avoid negative or critical individuals who bring you down or make you doubt yourself.

7. Set achievable goals: Break down larger goals into smaller, more achievable steps. This can help you

build confidence as you make progress and see results.

8. Get feedback: Seek feedback from trusted colleagues or mentors to get an outside perspective on your strengths and areas for improvement. This can help you gain a more objective view of your abilities and build confidence in your skills.

9. Embrace failure: Recognize that failure is a natural part of the learning process and an opportunity for growth. Instead of dwelling on mistakes, use them as a chance to learn, adapt, and improve.

10. Build a support network: Surround yourself with positive and supportive individuals who believe in you and your business. Seek out networking opportunities or join business groups to connect with other entrepreneurs and build a sense of community.

11. Practice visualization: Visualize yourself succeeding in a challenging situation, whether it's giving a presentation, closing a deal, or leading a team. This technique can help you build confidence and reduce anxiety.

12. Celebrate your uniqueness: Recognize and celebrate what makes you and your business unique. Embrace your individuality and use it as a competitive advantage.

13. Take action: Taking action, even if it's small steps, can help build momentum and increase confidence. Don't wait for everything to be perfect before taking action. Instead, focus on making progress and learning along the way.

3-How do I learn from mistakes.

Learning from mistakes is an essential part of personal and professional growth. Here are some steps you can take to effectively learn from your mistakes:

1. Own your mistakes: Take responsibility for your mistakes and avoid making excuses or blaming others. This can help you build trust with others and avoid repeating the same mistakes in the future.

2. Analyze what went wrong: Take time to reflect on what went wrong and why. Identify the factors that contributed to the mistake and consider what you could have done differently.

3. Accept the emotions: Acknowledge and accept any negative emotions that arise, such as frustration, disappointment, or embarrassment. Allow yourself

to feel these emotions without dwelling on them or letting them consume you.Eventually you can just ignore them.

4. Identify the lessons: Identify the lessons that you can learn from the mistake. Consider how you can apply these lessons to future situations and use them as opportunities for growth.

5. Make a plan: Develop a plan to avoid making similar mistakes in the future. Consider what actions you can take to prevent the mistake from happening again and what steps you can take to mitigate the consequences.

6. Implement the plan: Take action to implement the plan and put the lessons you've learned into practice. Hold yourself accountable and monitor your progress to ensure that you're making progress towards your goals.

7. Forgive yourself: Be kind and forgiving to yourself. Remember that mistakes are a natural part of the learning process, and everyone makes them. Avoid dwelling on the mistake or beating yourself up over it. As I said before eliminate any dwelling on negative thoughts just by visualizing those thoughts being consumed by fire.

By following these steps, you can effectively learn from your mistakes and use them as opportunities for growth and improvement. Remember that mistakes are a natural part of the learning process, and by approaching them with a growth mindset, you can turn them into valuable lessons.

Here are some more examples of ways to learn from mistakes:

8. Seek feedback: Seek feedback from others, such as colleagues, mentors, or trusted friends, to gain a different perspective on the mistake. This can help you identify blind spots or areas for improvement that you may have missed on your own.

9. Keep a journal: Keep a journal or log of mistakes you've made, what you learned, and how you plan to avoid similar mistakes in the future. This can help you track your progress and stay accountable.

10. Focus on solutions: Instead of dwelling on the mistake, focus on finding solutions and taking action to prevent similar mistakes in the future. This can help you maintain a positive and proactive mindset.

11. Analyse both success and failures: Analyse both successes and failures to understand what contributed to each outcome. By examining both,

you can identify patterns and behaviours that lead to success and those that lead to mistakes.

Remember, learning from mistakes is a continuous process. By incorporating these examples into your daily routine, you can gradually develop a growth mindset and use mistakes as opportunities for learning and growth.

4- How do I focus on the big picture

Focusing on the big picture is essential for achieving long-term success in business. Here are some steps you can take to help you stay focused on the big picture:

1. Define your goals: Define your long-term goals and break them down into smaller, more manageable steps. This can help you create a roadmap for

achieving your goals and stay focused on the bigger picture.

2. Prioritize your tasks: Prioritize your tasks based on their level of importance and how they contribute to your long-term goals. This can help you stay focused on the most critical tasks and avoid getting bogged down by smaller, less important tasks.

3. Avoid distractions: Identify and avoid distractions that can pull you away from the bigger picture, such as social media, email, or non-essential tasks. Consider setting boundaries or using time-management techniques to minimize distractions and stay focused.

4. Track your progress: Regularly track your progress towards your long-term goals to stay motivated and focused. This can help you see the progress you've

made and identify areas where you may need to adjust your strategy.

5. Think ahead: Consider how your actions today will impact your long-term goals. This can help you make decisions that are aligned with your bigger picture and avoid short-term thinking.

6. Seek feedback: Seek feedback from others, such as mentors or trusted colleagues, to gain a different perspective on your goals and strategy. This can help you identify blind spots and areas for improvement.

8. Visualize success: Take time to visualize what success looks like for you and your business. This can help you stay motivated and focused on your long-term goals, even during difficult times.

9. Break down complex tasks: Complex tasks can be overwhelming and make it challenging to focus on

the big picture. Break down larger projects into smaller, more manageable tasks, which can help you stay focused and make steady progress.

10. Celebrate successes: Take time to celebrate your successes and milestones along the way. This can help you stay motivated and focused on your long-term goals and remind you of the progress you've made.

11. Stay inspired: Seek out inspiration from others, such as successful entrepreneurs, industry leaders, or thought leaders in your field. Reading books, attending conferences, or listening to podcasts can help you stay motivated and focused on your long-term goals.

12. Define your purpose: Having a clear purpose or mission statement can help guide your decisions and keep you focused on your long-term goals. Take time to

define your purpose and make sure your actions align with it.

13.Embrace change: In today's fast-paced business environment, change is constant. Embrace change as an opportunity to learn and adapt to new situations, rather than as a threat to your long-term goals.

14.Create a long-term vision: Think beyond the next quarter or year and create a long-term vision for your business. This can help you stay focused on the bigger picture and make decisions that support your long-term goals.

15.Delegate effectively: As your business grows, you'll need to delegate tasks to others to focus on the bigger picture. Learn how to delegate effectively to ensure that important tasks are being completed while you focus on strategic planning.

16. Develop a plan for growth: Create a plan for how you will grow your business over time. This can include strategies for expanding into new markets, introducing new products or services, or acquiring other businesses.

17. Stay true to your values: Staying focused on the big picture means staying true to your values and vision for your business. Make sure that your actions align with your values and that you're building a business that reflects your long-term goals and aspirations.

By incorporating these points into your approach, you can stay focused on the bigger picture and build a successful business over the long term. Remember that staying focused on the big picture is a continuous process, and it requires ongoing effort and commitment.

5-How do I develop the ability to take constructive criticism

Developing the ability to take constructive criticism can be challenging, but here are some tips to help you:

1. Reframe your mindset: Try to view constructive criticism as an opportunity to learn and grow, rather than as a personal attack. Remember that nobody is perfect, and everyone has room for improvement.

2. Listen actively: When receiving criticism, take the time to listen actively to the person providing the

feedback. Avoid becoming defensive or interrupting them, and try to fully understand their perspective.

3. Ask questions: Ask questions to clarify any points that are unclear, and seek specific examples of how you can improve. This can help you better understand the feedback and make positive changes.

4. Focus on solutions: Instead of dwelling on the criticism itself, focus on finding solutions to the issues raised. This can help you take constructive steps to improve your performance or behavior.

5. Take time to reflect: After receiving constructive criticism, take time to reflect on what you've heard. Consider how you can apply the feedback to improve your performance or behavior, and make a plan to move forward.

6. Seek feedback regularly: To become more comfortable with constructive criticism, seek

feedback regularly from others. This can help you learn and grow over time and become more comfortable with receiving feedback.

7. Avoid taking criticism personally: Constructive criticism is not a reflection of your personal worth or value. Try to separate your self-worth from the feedback you receive.

8. Acknowledge your emotions: Receiving criticism can be emotionally challenging, and it's okay to feel upset or frustrated. However, it's important to acknowledge your emotions and process them in a healthy way, without letting them under your elephant skin.

9. Practice active listening: When receiving feedback, practice active listening by paying attention to nonverbal cues, asking clarifying questions, and

paraphrasing what you hear to ensure that you understand the feedback correctly.

10. Look for patterns: If you receive similar feedback from multiple sources, take note of any patterns. This can help you identify areas for improvement and make positive changes.

By incorporating these tips into your approach, you can become more comfortable with receiving constructive criticism and use it to improve your performance or behaviour over time. Remember that taking feedback is a valuable skill, and it can help you grow both personally and professionally.

6-How do I build resilience

Building resilience is an important skill that can help you navigate through challenging times and bounce back from setbacks. Here are some tips to help you build resilience:

1. Cultivate a growth mindset: Embrace challenges as opportunities to learn and grow. Instead of focusing on the negative aspects of a setback, try to see it as a chance to develop new skills or perspectives.

2. Practice mindfulness: Mindfulness practices, such as meditation or deep breathing, can help you manage stress and build resilience. Incorporate mindfulness into your daily routine to help you stay centered and focused.

3. Set realistic goals: Setting achievable goals can help you build confidence and a sense of accomplishment. Start with small goals and

gradually work your way up to more challenging ones.

4. Build your problem-solving skills: Developing strong problem-solving skills can help you navigate through challenging situations and find creative solutions to problems.

5. Stay optimistic: Cultivate a positive outlook and look for the good in situations. Try to focus on the things that you have control over, rather than dwelling on things that are beyond your control.Burn negative thoughts.

6. Learn from past experiences: Reflect on past challenges and setbacks and identify the strategies that worked well for you. Use this knowledge to build your resilience and develop new coping skills.

7. Build a strong social network: Surround yourself with positive, supportive people who can offer encouragement and help you stay motivated.

8. Stay flexible: Be willing to adapt to changing circumstances and adjust your approach as needed. This can help you remain resilient and stay focused on your goals.

9. Take care of your mental health: Seek professional help if you are struggling with depression, anxiety, or other mental health issues. Taking care of your mental health is an important part of building resilience.

10. Take breaks and practice relaxation techniques: Give yourself permission to take breaks and engage in activities that you find relaxing, such as reading, taking a walk, or listening to music. This can help you recharge and build resilience.

Remember that building resilience is a process that takes time and practice. By incorporating these tips into your daily routine, you can develop the skills and mindset needed to navigate through challenging times and bounce back from setbacks.

7-How do I learn to be persistent

Persistence is the ability to keep going even when faced with obstacles or setbacks. Here are some tips to help you learn to be more persistent:

1. Set clear goals: Define your goals clearly and make sure they are achievable. This can help you stay

focused and motivated, even when faced with obstacles.

2. Develop a plan: Break your goals down into smaller, more manageable tasks and develop a plan to achieve them. Having a clear plan can help you stay organized and motivated.

3. Stay positive: Cultivate a positive outlook and focus on the progress you have made, rather than dwelling on setbacks or failures.

4. Take action: Don't wait for things to happen – take action and make things happen. This can help you build momentum and stay motivated.

5. Be adaptable: Be willing to adjust your approach as needed and try new strategies if things aren't working.

6. Seek feedback: Seek feedback from others and be open to constructive criticism. This can help you identify areas for improvement and stay motivated.

7. Learn from failures: Instead of dwelling on failures, use them as opportunities to learn and grow. Identify what went wrong and develop a plan to avoid making the same mistake in the future.

8. Stay motivated: Find ways to keep yourself motivated, such as setting up rewards for yourself when you achieve certain milestones or surrounding yourself with supportive people who encourage you to keep going.

9. Stay organized: Use tools like to-do lists, calendars, and reminders to help you stay on track and avoid becoming overwhelmed.

10. Break tasks down into smaller steps: When faced with a large or complex task, break it down into

smaller, more manageable steps. This can make it feel less daunting and help you stay focused.

11. Visualize success: Take time to visualize yourself achieving your goals and enjoying the benefits of your hard work. This can help you stay motivated and focused on your end goal.

12. Embrace discomfort: Persistence often requires stepping out of your comfort zone and taking risks. Embrace discomfort and view it as an opportunity to learn and grow.

13. Practice self-discipline: Develop the discipline to stick to your plan and follow through on your commitments, even when you don't feel like it.

14. Stay focused: Keep your attention focused on your goals and avoid getting side-tracked by distractions or unrelated tasks.

15.Learn to manage stress: Stress can be a major obstacle to persistence. Practice stress-management techniques like meditation, exercise, or deep breathing to help you stay calm and focused.

16.Practice patience: Persistence requires patience and a willingness to keep going, even when progress seems slow. Recognize that achieving your goals may take time and effort, and be willing to stick with it.

17.Find a mentor: Seek out someone who has already achieved the kind of success you are aiming for and learn from their experience. This can help you stay motivated and learn valuable strategies for achieving your goals.

Remember that building persistence is a process, and it may take time to develop this skill. However, with dedication and practice, you can learn to stay motivated, focused, and persistent in the face of challenges and obstacles.

8-How do I practice mindfullness

Here are some steps you can take to practice mindfulness:

1. Set aside time: Schedule a specific time each day to practice mindfulness. This could be in the morning, during a break at work, or in the evening before bed.

2. Find a quiet place: Find a quiet place where you won't be disturbed, and where you feel comfortable and relaxed.

3. Sit comfortably: Sit comfortably in a chair or on the floor, with your back straight and your hands resting in your lap.

4. Focus on your breath: Close your eyes and focus your attention on your breath. Notice the sensation of the air moving in and out of your body.

5. Stay present: As you focus on your breath, your mind may wander. When this happens, gently bring your attention back to your breath, without judgment.

6. Be aware of your thoughts and feelings: As you practice mindfulness, be aware of any thoughts, feelings, or sensations that arise. Observe them without judgment, and then let them go.

7. Practice regularly: The more you practice mindfulness, the easier it will become. Aim to practice for at least 10-15 minutes each day, and gradually increase the duration over time.

8. Practice mindfulness in daily activities: Try to bring mindfulness to your daily activities, such as eating, walking, or washing dishes. Focus on the present moment and the sensations you are experiencing.

Remember that mindfulness is a skill that takes practice to develop. By incorporating these steps into your daily routine, you can cultivate mindfulness and experience the benefits of greater focus, clarity, and peace of mind.

Here are some additional tips to help you practice mindfulness:

9. Use guided meditations: Guided meditations can be helpful for beginners who are just starting to practice mindfulness. You can find a variety of guided meditations online or through meditation apps.

10.   Practice gratitude: Take a few moments each day to reflect on the things you are grateful for. This can help cultivate a positive mindset and reduce stress and anxiety.

11.   Practice self-compassion: Be kind and compassionate towards yourself as you practice mindfulness. Recognize that it is normal for your mind to wander, and that this is an opportunity to practice bringing your attention back to the present moment.

12.   Engage your senses: Engage your senses by noticing the sights, sounds, smells, tastes, and sensations around you. This can help bring

you into the present moment and increase your awareness.

13.   Be patient: Remember that mindfulness is a practice, and that it takes time to develop. Be patient with yourself and trust the process.

By incorporating these tips into your mindfulness practice, you can deepen your understanding and experience of mindfulness. With regular practice, you may find that mindfulness becomes a natural part of your daily routine, helping you to stay focused, calm, and centered in the present moment.

10-How do I learn to delegate

Learning to delegate effectively is an important skill for any leader or manager. Here are some steps you can take to improve your delegation skills:

1. Identify the tasks that can be delegated: Start by identifying tasks that can be delegated to others. These might be tasks that are not critical to your core responsibilities or that can be completed by someone with less experience.

2. Choose the right person for the task: When delegating tasks, it is important to choose the right person for the job. Consider the person's skills, experience, and workload, as well as their willingness to take on the task.

3. Communicate clearly: When delegating tasks, be clear about your expectations and instructions. Make sure the person understands the task, the deadline, and any specific requirements or guidelines.

4. Provide support: Be available to answer questions and provide support as needed. Offer guidance and feedback to help the person succeed in the task.

5. Trust the person: Delegation involves trusting someone else to complete a task or project. Trust that the person has the skills and resources to complete the task, and give them the autonomy to do so.

6. Follow up: Check in regularly to see how the task is progressing, and offer feedback and support as needed. Provide recognition and praise for a job well done.

7. Learn from the experience: Delegation is a learning process. Take the time to reflect on what worked well and what could be improved, and use this knowledge to improve your delegation skills in the future.

By following these steps, you can learn to delegate effectively and empower others to contribute to your team's success.

Here are some additional tips to help you improve your delegation skills:

8. Define clear boundaries: Clearly define the boundaries of the delegated task to avoid confusion and ensure that the person knows their responsibilities and authority.

9. Avoid micromanaging: Resist the urge to micromanage or take over the task once it has been delegated. This can demotivate the person and undermine their confidence.

10. Be flexible: Be open to different approaches and ways of doing things. Allow the person to use their own judgment and creativity to complete the task.

11.   Provide training and resources: Provide any necessary training, resources, or tools that the person may need to complete the task successfully.

12.   Prioritize tasks: Prioritize tasks based on their importance and urgency, and delegate accordingly. This can help ensure that critical tasks are completed on time and with the necessary level of attention.

13.   Be patient: Delegation can take time and effort to master. Be patient with yourself and with others as you work to improve your delegation skills.

Remember that delegation is not only about freeing up your time but also about empowering others to take on new challenges and develop new skills. With practice and commitment, you can learn to delegate effectively and achieve better results as a leader or manager.

How do I teach myself to stay adaptable

Staying adaptable is a valuable skill that can help you navigate change, uncertainty, and challenges in your personal and professional life. Here are some tips to help you teach yourself to stay adaptable:

1. Embrace change: Start by embracing change as a natural part of life. Accept that change is

inevitable and that adapting to new situations is necessary for growth and success.

2. Practice flexibility: Practice being flexible and open-minded in your approach to different situations. Be willing to adjust your plans and strategies as needed, and be open to new ideas and perspectives.

3. Build resilience:as elaborated previously build resilience by developing a positive mindset and a strong sense of self. Focus on your strengths, set realistic goals, and celebrate your successes.

4. Stay informed: Stay informed about changes and trends in your industry or field. Read industry news and blogs, attend conferences

and events, and network with colleagues to stay up to date.

5. Take calculated risks: Take calculated risks by trying new things and stepping outside of your comfort zone. This can help you develop new skills and perspectives, and build your confidence in adapting to change.

6. Practice mindfulness: Practice mindfulness techniques like deep breathing, meditation, and visualization to help you stay calm and centered in the face of change and uncertainty.

7. Seek feedback: Seek feedback from others, including colleagues, friends, and mentors, to

help you identify areas where you can improve and adapt.

Remember that staying adaptable is a process that requires ongoing effort and practice. By incorporating these tips into your daily routine, you can develop the skills and mindset needed to adapt to new situations and succeed in a rapidly changing world.

Here are some additional tips to help you stay adaptable:

9. Embrace diversity: Be open to different perspectives and ways of thinking. Diversity can

bring new ideas and approaches that can help you adapt to different situations.

10. Build a strong support network: Build a strong support network of friends, family, and colleagues who can provide encouragement, advice, and support during times of change and uncertainty.

11. Learn new skills: Continuously learn new skills and acquire new knowledge that can help you adapt to changing situations. Attend workshops, read books, and take online courses to stay up to date on industry trends and best practices.

12.   Take breaks: Take regular breaks and allow yourself time to rest and recharge. This can help you stay focused, motivated, and adaptable.

13.   Stay organized: Stay organized and prioritize your tasks to help you stay on top of your responsibilities and adapt to changing priorities.

Remember that staying adaptable is not only about responding to change but also about proactively seeking out new opportunities and taking risks. By adopting a growth mindset and focusing on continuous learning and improvement, you can develop the skills and resilience needed to succeed in

any situation.

11-How do I learn to set boundaries

Setting boundaries is an important skill that can help

you establish healthy relationships and protect your

time, energy, and emotional well-being. Here are

some tips to help you learn to set boundaries:

1. Identify your needs: Start by identifying your

    needs and priorities. Consider what's important

    to you and what you're willing and not willing

    to tolerate in your personal and professional

    relationships.

2. Communicate clearly: Communicate your boundaries clearly and assertively, using "I" statements to express your needs and expectations. Be direct and specific about what you need and what you're willing to do or not do.

3. Be consistent: Be consistent in enforcing your boundaries. If someone crosses a boundary, calmly but firmly remind them of your limits and stick to your boundaries.

4. Practice self-care: Practice self-care to help you build your confidence and resilience in setting boundaries. Take care of your physical and

emotional needs, and prioritize activities that help you feel happy and fulfilled.

5. Seek support: Seek support from friends, family, or a therapist if you need help setting and enforcing boundaries. Talking to others can help you gain perspective and build your confidence in setting boundaries.

6. Learn to say "no": Learn to say "no" when someone asks you to do something that goes against your boundaries or priorities. Saying "no" can be difficult, but it's an essential part of setting boundaries and taking care of yourself.

7. Practice boundary-setting in small ways: Start small by setting boundaries in low-stakes

situations, such as saying "no" to a social invitation that you're not interested in. As you become more comfortable, you can gradually set more complex boundaries.

Remember that setting boundaries is a skill that requires practice and patience. It's not always easy, but it's essential for maintaining healthy relationships and protecting your well-being. By taking the time to identify your needs, communicate clearly, and practice self-care, you can develop the skills and confidence needed to set and enforce boundaries in your personal and professional life.

Here are some additional tips for learning to set boundaries:

8. Be willing to compromise: While it's important to stand firm on your boundaries, it's also important to be willing to compromise when necessary. Consider alternative solutions or compromises that may work for both parties.

9. Avoid people-pleasing: Don't let the fear of disappointing others or being disliked prevent you from setting boundaries. Remember that setting boundaries is not selfish, but rather an important part of maintaining healthy relationships.

10.   Learn to handle pushback: Be prepared to handle pushback or resistance from others when you set boundaries. Practice responding calmly and assertively, and avoid becoming defensive or aggressive.

11.   Learn from experience: Use past experiences as learning opportunities to identify what worked and what didn't when setting boundaries. Reflect on what you could do differently next time, and adjust your approach accordingly.

12.   Set consequences: Set consequences for when boundaries are crossed, and follow through with them. This helps reinforce your

boundaries and sends a message that you take them seriously.

Remember that setting boundaries is a process that takes time and practice. It's normal to experience some discomfort or pushback at first, but with time and practice, you can develop the skills and confidence needed to set and enforce healthy boundaries in your personal and professional life.

12-How do I learn to seek support

Seeking support can be difficult for some people, but it's an important skill that can help you build resilience, cope with stress, and maintain healthy relationships. Here are some tips to help you learn to

seek support:

1. Recognize the importance of support:

   Understand that seeking support is not a sign

   of weakness, but rather a sign of strength. It

   takes courage to ask for help and reach out to

   others.

2. Identify your support network: Identify the

   people in your life who can provide emotional

   support, such as friends, family, colleagues, or a

   therapist. Make a list of these people and their

   contact information.

3. Be specific: When seeking support, be specific

   about what you need and what you're

struggling with. This will help your support network understand how they can best help you.

4. Ask for help: Reach out to your support network and ask for help when you need it. Be honest and open about what you're going through, and let them know how they can support you.

5. Listen to feedback: Be open to feedback from your support network. They may have insights or perspectives that you haven't considered, and their feedback can help you grow and learn.

6. Practice reciprocity: Remember that seeking support is a two-way street. Be willing to offer support to others in your network when they need it.

7. Seek professional help if needed: If you're struggling with a mental health issue or other serious problem, don't hesitate to seek professional help. A therapist or mental health professional can provide additional support and guidance.

Remember that seeking support is an ongoing process. It's important to prioritize relationships and build a support network that you can turn to in times of need. By being open, honest, and willing to seek and offer support, you can build stronger

relationships and develop the resilience needed to

navigate life's challenges.

13-How do I realize my mental toughness potential

Realizing your mental toughness potential requires

intentional effort and practice. Here are some steps

you can take to develop your mental toughness:

1. Set clear goals: Identify what you want to

   achieve and set specific, measurable, and

achievable goals. This will help you stay focused and motivated when faced with challenges.

2. Develop a growth mindset: Cultivate a mindset that sees challenges and failures as opportunities for growth and learning. Embrace the idea that your abilities can be developed through hard work and dedication.

3. Practice self-reflection: Take time to reflect on your experiences and emotions. Identify your strengths and weaknesses, and work on developing a better understanding of your mental and emotional state.

4. Cultivate resilience: Resilience is the ability to bounce back from setbacks and challenges.

Cultivate resilience by practicing self-care,

building a support network, and developing

coping skills.

5. Embrace discomfort: Mental toughness requires

a willingness to push past your comfort zone.

Challenge yourself by taking on new

experiences or pushing yourself in areas where

you feel uncomfortable.

6. Focus on the present moment: Develop

mindfulness practices to help you stay focused

on the present moment. This can help you stay

calm and centered in the face of challenges.

7. Practice positive self-talk: Your internal dialogue

can have a big impact on your mental

toughness. Practice positive self-talk, and reframe negative self-talk into more constructive and empowering messages.

Remember that developing mental toughness is a process that takes time and practice. By setting clear goals, cultivating a growth mindset, practicing self-reflection, building resilience, embracing discomfort, focusing on the present moment, and practicing positive self-talk, you can realize your mental toughness potential and achieve your goals.

Here are a few more tips to help you develop your mental toughness:

8. Create a plan of action: Mental toughness involves taking action, so create a plan that outlines the steps you need to take to achieve your goals. This will help you stay focused and motivated, and give you a roadmap for achieving success.

9. Build a support network: Surround yourself with positive, supportive people who encourage and motivate you. This can include friends, family members, mentors, or coaches.

10. Challenge yourself: Mental toughness requires pushing yourself beyond your limits. Set challenging goals and take on new

experiences that stretch your abilities and force you to grow.

11.   Stay optimistic: Optimism is an important part of mental toughness. Cultivate a positive outlook by focusing on the good in situations, expressing gratitude, and visualizing success.

12.   Practice self-discipline: Mental toughness requires self-discipline, which means developing the ability to stick to your goals and make choices that align with your values. Practice self-discipline by setting boundaries, establishing routines, and prioritizing your time.

Remember, mental toughness is not about being invincible or never experiencing fear or doubt. It's about developing the resilience and mindset needed

to overcome challenges and achieve your goals. By

taking intentional steps to build mental toughness,

you can achieve success and fulfillment in all areas of

your life.

how do I achieve self discipline

Achieving self-discipline requires effort and

commitment, but it is an essential skill for success in

any area of life. Here are some steps you can take to

develop self-discipline:

1. Set clear goals: Identify the specific goals you

   want to achieve and write them down. This

helps you stay focused and motivated, and gives you a clear sense of direction.

2. Create a plan: Break down your goals into smaller, achievable steps and create a plan for how you will reach them. This helps you stay organized and on track.

3. Prioritize: Determine what tasks are most important and prioritize them. Focus your energy and attention on the tasks that will have the most significant impact on your goals.

4. Eliminate distractions: Identify the distractions that pull you away from your goals and create a plan to minimize or eliminate them. This might

mean turning off your phone or blocking certain websites during work hours.

5. Develop a routine: Create a daily routine that includes time for work, exercise, self-care, and other important tasks. Having a routine helps you establish good habits and stay on track.

6. Hold yourself accountable: Take responsibility for your actions and hold yourself accountable for achieving your goals. Set up a system of rewards and consequences to motivate yourself to stay on track.

7. Practice self-control: Practice delaying gratification and resisting temptations that distract you from your goals. This helps you

develop the self-control needed to stay focused and disciplined.

Remember, self-discipline is a skill that can be developed with practice and persistence. By taking intentional steps to develop self-discipline, you can achieve greater success and fulfillment in all areas of your life.

Here are some additional tips for developing self-discipline:

1. Start small: Don't overwhelm yourself with too many goals or tasks at once. Start with small

steps and gradually increase your level of difficulty.

2. Focus on progress, not perfection: Don't be too hard on yourself if you slip up or make mistakes. Focus on the progress you've made and learn from your mistakes to improve in the future.

3. Find motivation: Identify what motivates you and use it to fuel your self-discipline. This might be a reward for achieving a goal or a reminder of why your goal is important to you.

4. Practice mindfulness: Mindfulness practices like meditation or deep breathing can help you

develop the self-awareness and self-control needed for self-discipline.

5. Get support: Surround yourself with supportive people who encourage you to stay on track and hold you accountable. Joining a support group or working with a coach or mentor can also be helpful.

6. Learn from others: Study the habits and routines of successful people who have strong self-discipline. Take note of what works for them and try to incorporate those practices into your own life.

Remember, developing self-discipline takes time and practice. Be patient with yourself, stay committed to your goals, and celebrate your successes along the way. With persistence and dedication, you can achieve the self-discipline needed to reach your full potential and develop your elephant skin for business.

www.ingramcontent.com/pod-product-compliance
Lightning Source LLC
Chambersburg PA
CBHW071027220526
45467CB00004B/1551